A COMPLETE EDITION OF
THE PAINTINGS
OF HIERONYMUS BOSCH

PHAIDON

HIERONYMUS BOSCH

THE PAINTINGS

COMPLETE EDITION

WITH AN INTRODUCTION

BY CARL LINFERT

EIGHTY ILLUSTRATIONS
INCLUDING TWENTY-FOUR
IN FULL COLOUR

PHAIDON PUBLISHERS INC
DISTRIBUTED BY DOUBLEDAY AND COMPANY INC
GARDEN CITY · NEW YORK

LAY-OUT OF THE PLATES BY LUDWIG GOLDSCHEIDER

TRANSLATED FROM THE GERMAN
BY JOAN SPENCER

MADE IN GREAT BRITAIN
PRINTED BY HUNT BARNARD & CO · LTD
AT THE SIGN OF THE DOLPHIN · AYLESBURY · BUCKS

INTRODUCTION

SINCE the first World War the paintings of Hieronymus Bosch have been studied, if not with increasing perceptivity, at least with increasing attention, and within easily definable limits. In some quarters he is regarded as a painter of the monstrous, of spectral menace, of nightmarish torture, or simply of the diabolical; but no sooner does this latter word appear (one still hears much talk of *diableries*) than it requires clarification. Gone is the late medieval hobgoblin, long since become a grotesque animal caricature not to be taken seriously, and instead – 'modern' even to the mind of the period – we have a monster carefully pieced together, in fact assembled from insects, reptiles, truncated human limbs and mechanical components. In a word, such a devil no longer fitted exactly into the representations of holy scripture, and was itself no longer a religious symbol. At a further stage Bosch's world, abounding in acts of violence and in discoveries, was seen as a series of pictorial tracts which appeared moral and reforming in intent, while they seemed also the product of a mystic's absorption or an alchemist's curiosity with its implied hope of universal metamorphosis. Recently, and this marks a still further stage, these pictures were thought to be inspired by the doctrines of a fraternity of 'Freethinkers', one of the manifold phenomena of pre-Reformation sectarian Christianity.

Those are the various stages of discovery, and each one discloses something of the essential Bosch. But none of these viewpoints renders any easier the task of assessing his work on its artistic merit, as the product of a painter's imaginative insight. This difficulty, now as always, is bound up with the description of the pictures themselves.

The first step, even the first complete examination of the pictures, is easy; what is difficult, as if that were Bosch's secret desire, will be to put into words what we see. But we do sense the period with all its upheavals, doubts and fears; we can see it in the paintings. I refer to the decades before the Reformation, when Bosch lived. Nothing is known of his personal life. There is only the entry in the archives stating that from about 1480 he lived and worked in 's Hertogenbosch, a little town in North Brabant, where he died in 1516. Since his family was formerly called 'Van Aeken', they probably came originally from Aachen. Our Bosch may well have been born about 1450 in the town whose name he bore, but he probably acquired some knowledge on his travels in addition to the provincial art which flourished at home, otherwise there would

5

be no trace in his work of those 'antiquarian' influences (deriving from Jan van Eyck and the Flemish-Burgundian miniaturists) which are so often remarked on, and he would appear more as the successor of painters like Rogier and Bouts who had long since risen to fame. He lived too far from the centres of artistic activity.

Bosch was cut off from them by living where he did, but he also lived in an age of blurred outline and often of uncertain frontiers. That is the reason for so many weird events, so much confusion, particularly in religion which was dominated by eschatological hopes and damaged by a resurgence of esoteric knowledge. Bosch was less a product of this than an answer to it. That may explain the mingled attraction and horror we feel when looking at his paintings today. There were already enough formal peculiarities present in his sources of inspiration, Gerard David, the Master of the Virgo inter virgines and one or two others. But none of them used the remoulding of form to reveal fresh content so profoundly as did Bosch.

There were many straightforward methods of regarding this: as a dry, scurrilous jest, or perhaps as a cynical, amusing exercise in the diabolical, or merely as satire, as if this formal peculiarity was striving to contain everything it could. What of his form? It earned him the reputation of a bizarre visionary, causing first one then another stylistic tendency to be attributed to him. But attempts to do justice to the dignity of his forms finally forced them to be taken seriously. Tolnay, for example, saw in Bosch's forms a pictorial representation of Ruysbroek's mystical system of thought, but even this perceptive judgment did not escape the assumption that Bosch had illustrated something already a hundred years old. Or consider Fraenger's opinion that we have here a faithful representation of the procedures and ritual mode of life obtaining in the communities of 'Free-thinkers'. But how could even this be regarded as a fitting judgment on these paintings? As though they were a souvenir, a factual account or an idealisation of events in those communities, however remarkable they may have been. For these esoteric events constitute 'reality' and are the 'model' in precisely the same way as a landscape painter's raw material is the scene he paints; it still says nothing of the artistic quality of the pictures as a contrast or alternative version to reality.

Let us observe how Bosch's style is born and slowly develops into his characteristic manner. The dates are lacking which would permit any definite assertion of the chronological order of these pictures.

But the forms themselves, the style of painting which displays dull surfaces, virtuosity of brushwork, and finally a sublime, hidden tranquillity in the application of colour, do suggest a meaningful order. And this meaning, pursued for three decades in the researches of Baldass, Friedländer, Tolnay and Combe, produced a chronology which, with only slight divergences, gradually won the agreement of the connoisseurs.

No one could fail to regard the *Seven Deadly Sins* (Plates 1–6) and the *Cure of Folly* (Plates 7–8) as the earliest works. Both are roundels; the latter is a scene set against a landscape, but the former is a circular arrangement of the seven pictures which surround a tondo of Christ so as to form an eye, of which he is the pupil, the whole representing the eye of God. Four smaller tondos form the four corners of the *tabla* for which this painting is intended. Obviously these are pictures less to be contemplated than to be examined when in daily use. They are unskilfully executed but keenly observed. Their content is different from that of former scenes inserted between stories from the life of Christ or of the Saints and portraits of donors. They depict customs and incidents of daily life, not in the manner of later 'moral pictures', but noted as examples of virtues, vices or passions, and revealed in people just as chance does reveal them. Hitherto this had occurred only in Calendars and in illustrations of historical events which depicted in miniature form mythological or more modern campaigns alongside a wealth of secondary incident. But now the aim was totally different: anger, envy, slothful and futile daydreaming are shown in an aspect of such richness that we may observe here the source of Bosch's unexampled imaginative power. He is indeed more than the inventor of goblins who, according to a long established convention in the grotesque, pop out from behind the chest to scare the vain lady typifying Pride. Here one sees a completely new use made of that partial naturalism that had flourished so vigorously in the 14th century (but had been forgotten for fifty years, ever since the painter's vision had become completely naturalistic).

The painter is still a penetrating observer, but now he exposes something that almost eludes observation: the threat concealed behind actions, or even appearances alone. His penetrating vision opens the way to the first breath of menace which will later produce the fundamental features of Bosch's pictorial art: forebodings, temptation, despair and perdition. In the other picture, *Cure of Folly*, a cranial operation on an idiot, the threat comes rather from stupidity and charlatanism. Here is the birth of that delusion which obscures the truth and finally excludes it altogether. Foolish eagerness and idle pomposity, funnel and book on their heads –

these details produce an even more destructive effect on us when set against the broad landscape in which everything seems ordered in the most peaceful harmony. However, the *Conjurer* (Plate 9) is lurking in front of a blank wall and this group of people, taken in by the fraud or merely idly watching, is already a firmly welded piece of human machinery. It should be remembered that this element of human mechanism, not merely desires and fears, is one of Bosch's constant themes.

In the *Marriage at Cana* (Plate 12), another early work, the calm of a joyous occasion is marred by almost venomous overtones. A solemn, almost rigid company of guests (some of whom are anticipated in Bouts' work) appear oppressed by unknown ghostly influences. In the background stands a magician's altar: animals, to be eaten at table, snarl on their plates, while the spiteful croaking of an old crone's bagpipes (recurring so often in later pictures) dominates the scene. But it is not clear what is really going on: the ceremonial rite of a sect, or witchcraft invading the ceremony; for the picture has a double meaning however much one may interpret it. At all events the emotional content is sinister: suspicion, hypocrisy and secretiveness prevail right into the farthest corner. Even the colours seem to be an outer skin concealing something. In the *Ecce Homo* (Plates 14–15) the interest, unequally divided, is held by a no less suspicious crowd, this time packed tightly together. The contrast is important here too: the hard, obtrusive foreground gives place to a broad, placid scene of provincial life, its friendly atmosphere unruffled even by a mob of malcontents.

Among the early works the *Crucifixion* (Plate 13), the *Adoration of the Magi* (Plate 10), and the *Carrying of the Cross* (Plate 16) deserve mention because, while remaining faithful to the old style of composition, they have a new and arresting quality. These figures in their pale, almost smooth-rubbed attire, are remarkable not only because of this scantily cut garb (often almost the costume of malice itself); they also display fully both the brightness of colour and the concealing grey which characterized Bosch all his life. It was with the greater assurance that the hostile sentiments they heralded began to erupt and spread in the form of violent, rapid, angular movements – as in another *Carrying of the Cross* (Plate 17) which is still more sinister because here an irresistible torrent of people, branching off from the two scenes with the thieves, is crowded into a vertical format. Thus these wild, harrying forms which will be Bosch's element from now on, have started along the path leading to that picture which is their ultimate goal; they will soon be united with these elements of disquiet which had crept into Bosch's work long since.

8

But what are these elements? What is meant by 'disquiet'? Bosch's landscapes will seem more and more peaceful. They are firm and serene, but they contain an almost imperceptible presage. Are they undergoing a change? At least they seem to be holding their breath. Bosch actually 'sees' change. Something is emerging which is not yet manifest. Not the fleeting, disjointed aspect of events, but rather annihilation of incident which informs the whole and is the matrix of all isolated happenings. But, however well concealed, they are so deeply imprinted on these crowded canvases with their wealth of startling themes that (as in this *Carrying of the Cross*) the features not immediately apparent are the more potently suggestive.

The visible scene offered to us by Bosch always contains a question, a tempter's question. What is to happen? Or even, what *has* happened? Hence the many interpretations which Bosch always evokes. The problem will not be resolved at a single glance, still less in a single word. In each of his pictures a choice is offered. Even the choice of what you see in it. Is it Paradise or torment, the beginning of life or its end, possession by demons or their defeat by the penitent? – and many more choices which we shall shortly encounter. And finally there is revealed that delicate indecision inherent in all serious choices, which does after all constitute the partly straightforward, partly contradictory fabric of life. Is there any other reason why it is so difficult to decide whether Bosch was a heretic or just another orthodox if critical believer? It may be said that he paints stiff, petrified excrescences whose sole existence lies in his visions, but by means of these very creations Bosch has ingeniously captured and fixed the whole of life and the Day of Judgment, in all their beauty and deformity.

Anyone who studies Bosch's paintings will find, both in the earliest and the later ones, that 'questioning' mode of vision which always elicits from the world the unexpected and inexplicable. But this is no mere painter's sport; he illumines his territory of marvels with sharp highlights, themselves unexpected in their startling metamorphoses. Thus there is no solution of enigmas, but a probing of the multifid creatures in his pictures. But what is his method? Like an alchemist, contrary to all logic, but most magically, he shows in his curious problem pictures the countless opportunities of transformation, purification, conquest, which are taken or thrown away. *The Haywain* (Plates 19–24) is an examination of this kind. The first thing one notices is the scurrying, restless throng; for the picture's subject, the proverb, 'The world is a haystack: each man takes what he can snatch' promises nothing but violence between the wheels and under the load of hay. On closer examination the cart seems to be standing still like an allegorical triumphal chariot, respectfully followed by a cavalcade of the great ones of this world and crowned by a pair of lovers engrossed in their music and oblivious of all else. In fact this centralized, monstrance-like composition is itself the gruesome element. Precisely because of this calm, central arrangement this picture actually shows evil at work. The story is not static, it exists and yet still develops. Here we are shown that the directing force behind all these events is far removed from the picture. Is it Christian exhortation, or does the painter regard Christ in the clouds as the mischief-maker? That is a matter of preference, just as Bosch always shows that a real choice does exist between good and evil, angel and devil. The colours in this picture still have the same picture-sheet firmness as the early works; it belongs in fact to the decade before 1500.

In this painting the new type of devil, that combination of animal, plant and machinery, appears for the first time like a plaguing swarm of insects. And this many-headed monster attacks the head of the procession and pulls the cart along. Here we enter upon the road to perdition, which leads us over into the scene of destruction on the right-hand panel, a half-finished tower where flame and darkness mingle. The procession solemnly advancing in the rear suspects nothing, nor do the masses pouring out of an antheap as though from a trapdoor. This picture and all the succeeding ones plunge us into Bosch's element. Although, in a picture like *Death and the Miser* (Plate 26) this new type of demon is concealed and seems only to peep through the cracks, soon it will spread like a pestilence until, though not necessarily visible as a monster, it sets its mark even on the happy figures, distorting every visible object. Its source is here, in this double picture of congestion and stagnation, with its colours bespeaking both mellowness and devastation.

But if we are to absorb and savour this ingredient of Bosch's pictorial universe it is time to mention a process which permeates all his work. The hobgoblins, the weird figures, the disturbing influences, appear only to disappear again. First they were only faintly disguised. But even when their aspect was the same their place was different. During the 'Gothic' centuries preceding Bosch the appearance of the diabolical element in representations of Holy Scripture was governed by hard and fast rules. Devils had set scenes with strictly predetermined themes. But Bosch is no longer dominated by his subject. The action, whether sacred or diabolical, is not tied to any place, or at least its place is changed. The successors to these devils, as seen by Bosch, need no habitat; they plan the enterprise and the painter merely equips them. These monsters of his own invention, these phantasms put together as if under a microscope, have been loosed on the world, and now they rule it. Once merely symbols, they now engender a new significance; one might actually say, thanks to the methods invented by Bosch, and as such may have established an incomparable and entirely original arsenal of images. But these menacing, astounding creatures disappear once more, disclosing wide vistas apparently inviolate. That occurs in a few late works, where the world has in fact been transformed. In what way? It has assumed a calm, emerging from the most violent agitation, of which it still bears traces. Bosch, that most anguished of all painters, at length actually succeeded in painting beneath apparent serenity merely the traces of that disquiet which had been his own discovery; having introduced disturbance he now brings forth peace, or rather, being intent on the truth, he merely portrayed the after-effects of this peace. Few people noticed this deceptive calm which descends when the devils have departed – none so well as he. That was his 'discovery', or rather his observation. The first example of this calm amidst agitation (or let us say, calm bordering upon agitation), is the Lisbon Triptych, the most significant picture of temptation he ever produced – a temptation whose outcome is uncertain.

But between the devils' appearance and their disappearance we have lost sight of one procedure common to all these pictures, one which will always be regarded as peculiar to Bosch. I mean the arousing of happy desires alternating with torturing fear. The pictures succeed each other like a series of events showing how reality, having but recently received her form, comes under Bosch's weird influence, and is harried, whipped and cruelly ill-used. All Bosch's objects have also an immaterial quality; does this make reality appear alien, petrified and mechanical? Or does it not poison reality, making it pliable, weak and transparent? For indeed, from now on more and more of Bosch's visions are glassy and transparent. But what lies behind the transparency? All that appears is the object itself rendered transparent, but at the same time it hints at the absence of any further background or support. Thus in his own way Bosch creates and manifests a profundity that is merely veiled and disguised. But the enduring profundity of his paintings will be the way he looks ahead from the very heart of the Middle Ages and perceives the future in a mechanical view of the world totally lacking in his contemporaries' forms. For that very reason he anticipates so far ahead that it has been possible to compare his work, inadequately and superficially, with our current surrealist horror formulae. It was the more easy to interpret him (always unequivocally) as a mystic, an alchemist, a sectarian, every kind of heretic, in that he himself, dissatisfied with his own period, experimented with all its motifs. As a painter he is so great a spiritual innovator that he was never a programme painter either of ecclesiastical or secular subjects. This does not impair the partial validity of all the interpretations put upon his work.

We ought, however, to see him as he saw the world, and mistrust rigid formulae. He allowed every theme he touched to appear and then disappear, so that in the end Christians and non-Christians alike found themselves in the difficult land of the isolated individual. This faltering advance, this often imperceptible and yet ineluctable forward urge, was itself painful. Bosch never portrayed this process in his pictures dramatically but allowed it to be felt, like the hand of time. He painted like one with his eye on the clock, hard-pressed by the flight of time. This is apparent in the *Ship of the Fools* (Plate 27), a rigid picture of self-absorption. Who mans this craft, seeming to float on the sea, yet looking like an emanation from a swamp? Idiots, who treat everything senselessly, time more than anything. They exist, not in the world but in a vacuum. The bushy tree that serves them as a mast appears their one hold on reality. Yet it is a delusion, like the barge itself. They drift in happy abandon, no longer aware of their direction. But the real horror is their self-engrossment, further emphasized and rendered positively blatant by this constricted, vertical composition. This is in truth a cosmos sufficient unto itself, as if the real world were equally pointless. Is it not? Only people themselves can make it seem otherwise. But that implies people who do not look about them and are not beside themselves. Bosch was not yet painting contemplatives of that kind.

It must be realized that aimless drift and preoccupation with one's own outward behaviour constituted that madness in face of which he finally discovered these contemplatives. He actually conjured them up to stem the mad hordes. Christ was the supreme sacrifice; even exposed to the gaze of deepest scorn he could do no other than suffer. In the later *Ecce Homo* (Plate 28) he is almost obscured by the mass of wild, brazen, twitching faces of the scoffers. The picture is the most difficult of all to date. In my view the sharp angularity of the forms, selected with the delight of an expert in costume, serves to differentiate it from the crumpled draperies of the final Gothic phase. Thus despite all the jagged lines there results a smooth, almost unreal undulation which anticipates the non-muscular or the lean bony structure of his subsequent figures.

12

Over this pervasive smoothness is thrown a delicate film of splendour. It appears again in the *Crucifixion of Saint Julia* (Plate 29) with the same delicacy of surface. Now, whether this type of picture should be placed before or after the second of the three great triptychs (the Lisbon Triptych), they are certainly characteristic of the middle period of Bosch's life; only now will he begin to reveal the dominant motifs of his artistic visions. It is at least true of both these pictures that the delicately painted draperies seem to be a protection as well as the expression of deep sensibility. Despite the wealth of gesture in these paintings they also seem withdrawn into a significant exoticism, so that they could indeed both be styled *chinoiseries*. What an odd preparation for that 'weirdness' which Bosch is soon to make his own.

It would seem necessary from now on to observe a trick of style which will always find a place in Bosch's scenes, or upheavals (as all his pictures can be termed). I mean the encasing, the incapsulation, or in more normal phraseology, the concealment and imprisonment of the open form. It is often a thin mask stretched across like a skin, but sometimes the brittle casing has burst, as if everything around were about to disintegrate and fall to dust in the same way. This quality was not yet present in the *Haywain*. There one saw rather the remains of the rending and gnawing process which had been cast aside and left where they fell; moreover in that picture the danger lay in the solidly constructed tower, whereas elsewhere the threat comes from caverns and abysses. Nor is this quality very evident in the Vienna *Last Judgement* (Plates 48–49). Here no clear distinction exists between capsule, cage or cell, but the construction is firm throughout. There is not yet any sign of collapse or decay.

But other details, more smoothly incorporated in later works, stand out in sharper relief, particularly the mechanical activity, the tireless portrayal of torture, the delight in devices of indirect attack, dungeons, trapdoors, pits, together with the nocturnal fires that cleave the darkness with their flashing eyes. The innovation is the altar to St. Julia. That is the tree on the left that looks like a mountain cave. Even so, it is not yet the hollow shell it will more and more become in subsequent pictures. Rather does it seem a reminiscence of the old city gates of the Trecento paintings with their floods of people pouring through them, as here. But we sense in this tree-stump, as in the towers of the side panels, the quest for forms that might represent decaying natural growths as well as inflated constructions of clay and stone. Soon these forms will be discovered and this petrified dissolution will yield the fossilized remains of

13

alarming metamorphoses. Pictures of this type contain sections which may be regarded simply as monuments to the transforming fantasies of an alchemist.

But let us first examine the gleams of light, the cavities, the undulations in the four paintings of the Last Things in the Palace of the Doges (Plates 46–47). How many cavities there are, but how often are beams of light directed through these cavities! The *Fall of the Damned*, on the other hand, shows darting, blinding light in a jungle of darkness. And even the water, there behind the mountain where the fires persist, does not conduce to meditative calm; its reflected gleam alone becomes a fresh onslaught of terror. Nowhere is there a hint of that combination of fear, misery and almost withered hope to be found in the later pictures, even the bright ones. Thus it seems the more necessary to look first of all at this dark glittering sheen in Bosch's work. The clearest example of this close intermingling of light and dark is in the grisailles. They, too are a completely valid form of painting and in Bosch's hands particularly they reveal all the power of the painter's brush, even when he can command only the countless nuances of one neutral shade. The two panels *Before and after the Flood* (Plate 32) have always seemed to me the most powerful and the most implacable in conception. (One of them, according to Fraenger, represents the barbarous descendants of the fallen angels and their human brides, the other shows the descent from the Ark.) Everything is arid. At the foot of the Mountain of the Ark the ground is crisscrossed with runnels and channels, all dry and silted up; they embody (in such a grisaille) the painter's doubt whether fertility will ever return. The dominant mood of grey seems in itself to represent the insecure but resistant co-existence of mankind and the world. However it must be observed how rarely one finds a scene like *After the Flood* in Bosch's work, with its pictures of movement, advance and retreat. Here, on one single occasion, arrival is also portrayed. And yet those who are saved encounter the corpses left by the subsiding waters. That is their first moment of happiness: their former anxiety is dead, and time is reborn.

These two studies in grey contain caverns, truncated mountains and abysses. The hollow shell-like constructions we have already seen anticipated do not yet appear. Nor are they found on the grey outsides of the wings of the Lisbon altar-piece; we see two massive towering hump-backed mountains and the rest of the landscape slopes down towards us in a series of plateaux, giving the effect of a gently graduated staircase. But this panel perhaps more than any other reveals the virtuosity of the painter's brushwork, seen in fullest splendour on the right-hand panel of the *Carrying of the Cross*. And all those figures we once saw rushing and clattering, cursing and grinding their teeth, are now one great mob surging straight at us! There seems now to be less hatred but a still more inhuman coarseness and ruthlessness at work; even sheer indifference is there, masquerading as a good-natured stout woman of ample girth. This accentuates the lean incisiveness of the anguished male-factor scenes in the foreground, of the almost wasted skeleton of a starving beggar and an appalling decapitated head impaled on a spike. These are all examples of a fundamental horror and violence of incident without the slightest addition of the weird or the supernatural. But they occur on the inside of the altar-piece; the austerity of the outside warns us not to regard them merely as scurrilous or comic.

A further warning is given by the *Temptation of Saint Anthony* (Plates 33–45) which, together with the *Garden of Earthly Delights* is the most perfect and most animated of all Bosch's paintings, although, unlike the latter, it is painted in subdued colours. The capacity even of these colours to glow and impress themselves upon us is the more astonishing. And here too we see those hollow edifices and growths which form the labyrinthine haunts of lurking dangers.

One should always remember that, as the Middle Ages wear on, the widespread fear of evil spirits is increasingly transformed into a painful searching of conscience, not only in the devout but even more in critic-ally-minded doubters. This meticulous and thorough introspection is the ground from which phobias spring. The approach of the Reforma-tion with its tendencies to enlightenment brings a graver and more frequent awareness of the onslaughts of temptation. In fine: conscience and self-examination merely strengthen the grip of the supernatural. Bosch exteriorized this in his work; it was his concern, but he had already repudiated it.

The appalling definition of the monsters might for a moment make one ask whether they too are under attack and not merely Saint Anthony. However, he is in fact the victim, even though he and all his entourage appear secure on an island plateau in the face of the encompassing chasms and flood waters. But what has been saved? Surely nothing but this process of temptation and torture which, as here presented, holds scant prospect of relief. Here the 'island' is nothing but a remnant of the world. The left background, aglow with flame, is almost submerged by the rising flood. From this vantage point one can see what Bosch has painted: the direct conflict between light and its extinction, combustion and decay, fire and swamp, as though the Saint too had nothing but the

15

choice between dazzling blindness and suffocation. This, in its refined form, is the supernatural menace foreshadowed in the alchemists' writings, as the clash, the combination and the metamorphosis of the elements. But the forms chosen by Bosch for his separate, flesh-and-blood devils had been dimly guessed at by thousands, if perceived by none.

Thus it happens that, seen from these two aspects of the imagination, the supernatural assumes the seriousness of a rite, even if a blasphemous one. Bosch is himself no Satanist but an orthodox believer who, like many of his time, was capable of criticism. If he is a heretic then he is a heretic who, thanks to the power of his artistic imagination, had no desire whatever to see even the beginnings of a rival sect. That is why he painted the world as it was and might remain for a long time: encompassed by lurking destruction, the Saint borne along half dead, his one remaining desire to avert his anguished gaze from the dreadful, inescapable distortions and wanton perversions of actions which once, in a different setting, constituted a religious ceremony, or at least a serious gathering, but not a congregation of scoffers. The object of ridicule is the Saint, not the truth which must be sought after and hallowed. No curse is laid on the path which might lead to the truth; it falls instead upon the sectarian hypocrite with a swine's head, who chants from his gruesome blue psalter, and upon the sorcerer concealed behind the wall but recognizable by his tall hat. Both of them, stationed beneath Saint Anthony's platform, one to the right, and one to the left, are 'conducting' the general uproar. All the monsters, whether carrying a toad, an egg, a beaker or a tankard, are merely the blood-curdling horrors these two have conjured up.

The most striking feature about these creatures assembled here is their urge to creep off, shut themselves in, lock themselves away. However active they may be, their tortures always culminate in seclusion or mutilation. Everything seems to have crept into its shell, so that every incident seems concealed and sly. Observe the crawling giant on the left panel. How laboriously is he trying to force a way out of this cramping universe: an arrow strikes him down. Or see the depraved spectacle of the naked figures on the right panel, who juggle with a table bearing vessels of an uninviting and dubious nature, while the bloodstained tablecloth trails on the ground: but they too are threatened with murder and insanity.

Moreover the temptation scene seems cut off from the outer world too. In the distance (particularly between the buildings on the right panel) the landscape is serene. There the world seems secure, less threatened

16

than in the central panel, at all events tranquil. What an illusion! Evil symptoms point to trouble even there: the warlike crowds behind the wall, the sinking ships, the gigantic beacon on the mountain. Even the airborne chariots drawn by frogs and fishes deepen rather than relieve the horror.

It is only in the centre that the full effect of this concentrated temptation is felt. I do not refer to all those sinister apparitions so readily regarded as 'scurrilous', but to one single constantly recurring form: the hollow shell. These shells, usually the hollow trees, which half conceal something, which yawn, gape, moulder, are the first embodiments of entirely evil intent.

They cloak and yet disclose putrefaction, which itself poisons whatever remains alive. Tree spirits and half truncated skeletons are of this type. So is the cleft tree that shelters the temptress, herself another hollow shell. These are the hidden lairs of the unexpected. This is the source of the temptation. Illusion and truth join and speak with a double voice. The building with a crucifix in a niche is also of this type; half inviting, half enticing one into the uncertain darkness. It is a ruin of former glories. The outside wall with its reliefs showing the messengers bringing a grape from the Promised Land, together with a pagan sacrifice, Moses the law-giver in contrast to the idolaters of the golden calf, testifies to the days when good and evil were clearly distinguishable. The ruin itself is almost a hollow shell and from it a shaky path leads down across a bridge into the dark interior of a delicate, fragile, glassy edifice. The tower at the end looks both like a jug and a cave, while the whole construction closely resembles a jetty. It is impossible to tell whether it has any foundations or is merely floating. But the egg-shaped tower with its cylindrical-topped cupola protruding through its shattered end has draped itself in a mantle as if to conceal further deeds of darkness.

This picture has one example, possibly the first, of a huge bursting fruit from which has emerged the man with the horse's skull who plucks at his harp as he rides on a duck wearing shoes. Elsewhere we shall see this fruit disgorging figures of delight which are human, not supernatural. But the most remarkable aspect of the monstrous creatures on this Lisbon altar-piece is that there are no more devils in the hitherto accepted sense. They have been replaced by pieces of mechanism. Concealing arabesques usher in the technical age – the age of the supernatural. Such is the indirect influence on the picture of the alchemists' elemental magic. And that is why Bosch's style displays more and more explicitly this amalgam of living creatures and inanimate, man-made objects, however vivid and arresting. (I do not equate 'living' with 'organic', for even monsters like snakes and scorpions are organic.) But in return more and more objects assume the gestures of living people. They are, however, puppets, colourless *personae*, or even mere remains of human bodies which have been incorporated into a piece of apparatus. In the tank corps, and particularly in older armies, there is still room for individual valour and decisions taken on individual initiative. Bosch invents 'valiant' machines, not just engines of torture but actual living mechanisms. Even so they are manipulated by an unseen hand, a 'devil' if you will, but a devil Bosch now keeps concealed.

It would be mistaken to see in this an unlimited acceptance of the supernatural in the world. The limit is set by the temptation theme. The tempted Saint conquers and subdues the enemy. Bosch refuses to portray these vanquished monsters as a victorious, arbitrary force. And that is the attitude of the hermits Bosch is constantly painting. On the altar-piece of the *Hermits* (Plate 50) the panel devoted to Saint Anthony merely shows monstrous and fearful combinations of mangled limbs. Saint Jerome, in the centre, kneels at prayer on the crumbling remains of a splendid tessellated floor and is surrounded by the ruins of an ancient chapel, while the cave behind it is such a confusion of mingled mineral and plant life that the ruins themselves will eventually be swallowed up by this wilderness of vegetation. In the Ghent *Saint Jerome* (Plate 51) there is an even closer fusion of tree-roots and 'buildings' (in the form of scattered plinths), and there are no torturing ghouls. This is not a temptation scene but an act of penance for long-standing evil. Hence the intrinsic validity of the statement: all hermits, those who still wrestle with evil and those who do penance, are exorcists. This observation holds good if our initial assertion is true, namely that even the later pictures from which nearly all the devils have vanished, still retain their menace. Not only in Bosch's tortuous canvases completely overrun by demons, but throughout his work, the real subject matter is man's ability to endure them, drive them out and subdue them. This is also true of the solitary contemplatives who, like *Saint John on Patmos* (Plates 52–55) inhabit a peaceful sea-girt landscape, though here one isolated hint of temptation still remains. This bringer of confusion is himself an eloquent combination of insect, reptile and iron weapon, with a fuming explosive on his head, and an anxious human face. On the other hand, how different is the evilly rampant vegetation in *Saint John the Baptist in the Wilderness* (Plate 57). The thistle bearing the pomegranate sprouts from a narrow crevice in the rock. It also seems the signal for an episode of horror like the confused heap of doors and stone slabs in the background, with its wealth of trapdoors. Both branches and stone are uniformly grey. But the smooth figure lies as untroubled as the otherwise peaceful landscape. There are more isolated symptoms of unrest in the landscape of *Saint Christopher* (Plate 56). The Saint, a cloud of billowing folds, fords the river (to Fraenger, the 'River of Death') with that ardent half running, half leaning gait which recurs repeatedly in Bosch's work, but on either bank one sees symbols of vanity and force. Here, as in all of Bosch's pictures where there is advance, quest or merely aimless wandering, the lines of the composition are slanting (an entirely non-medieval trait). Each of the three last mentioned pictures conveys the impression that the entire landscape – apparently so tranquil – has become an enclosing envelope, an outer husk. But this only shows how irrevocably this enclosed form has become a fundamental pattern of his entire sensory perception, even when it is hidden from view.

Since this pattern implies both sides of every promise, as of the darkly mysterious, the concealed, the still fermenting elements in Bosch's work, it is possible not only to foresee but in part to explain its further development in the third of the great triptychs, *The Garden of Earthly Delights* (probably painted as early as the first decade of the sixteenth century, like the Lisbon Triptych). Here indeed is a gay theme set against a sinister background (Plates 58–67). I shall leave open the question of the picture's meaning. It may be the creation and decline of the world which is shown on the outside as a disc within a sphere, half-finished, but already putting out its menacing tentacles of luxuriant growth (Combe) or it may be a picture of the state of the world immediately before the millennium (Fraenger). Of course the obvious question is, how could this 'garden' be an altar-piece? A circumspect answer would probably be that it was not merely an altar-piece for a church but for specific side-chapels. At that period there were clerics who sought out highly detailed fantasies precisely to combat the unorthodox experimental pictures so insidiously prevalent. But the sects were more concerned with their plotting and planning than with accurate representations of these activities, and the first thing they would have destroyed would no doubt have been the firmest link, i.e. the purely formal, with traditional altar-painting, namely the triptych form.

Even if one did not regard the picture in a sectarian, unorthodox way as a representation of Paradise one had no need to call it a 'Warning against Lust'. Rather is it a combination of doubt and wish-fulfilment manifested in the creatures hesitating between the elements and finally eluding them, and shown also in other metamorphoses. Thus it is best described as a picture of the world in alchemical flux. Moreover at every point in the picture, in all the forms, gestures and movements, may be seen that hesitation, that magic expectancy, which correspond both to the character of the picture and to its subject. What in fact is happening here? What is being revealed? A nascent mode of vision, a choice and appraisal of forms accompanied by a most attractive tenderness and fragility. What other view could one take of the figure of Christ, shown at the creation of Eve and bathed in rosy light? He is merely a passive observer. Everything else seems poised before all action, in the timeless freedom of Paradise. Only the pool beneath, full of hybrid creatures still evolving is 'used'. An opposing world, with its concealments and its luxuriant growth (which always go hand in hand) is discernible only in the distance. But the 'building' in the centre hardly seems to have been deliberately 'erected'; this fount of life wells up in flesh-like tints and showers down its forms; it is fountain and flame in one, and shaped like a tabernacle. But what is beneath, just above the blueish mound of slime, the centre of the glass ball? Is it an eye or just a hollow shell? Is it something peering out or something growing through?

This is the picture on the main panel. It is a jungle of water and growth, with a wealth of shell-like concealments. These naked, delicate, plant-like bodies seem to insinuate themselves but hesitantly into the picture. The gaiety they embark on is suddenly extinguished as if by enchantment. Many appear fixed and immobile as though they had fallen full length and dropped asleep from voluptuousness. Even if these naked beings are no longer in life (according to an anthroposophic like Wertheim they are 'Soul bodies' shortly after death) yet their activities are what they were in life – with a new grace which looks quite different from real, normal sensuality, but which is the motive for an imaginative representation such as this. The painting is thus less a whirl of unconscious dream images than a daydream, full of richly, accurately painted, but evanescent costumes of desire.

Despite all the extravagance of incident, the composition of this picture and the landscape were planned with similar accuracy. Three zones may be distinguished. The further they recede the more they tend towards symmetry. The second revolves round a circle, the third, rectangular in arrangement, leads the eye along a perspective towards the horizon. The foreground, apart from the single mussel shell enclosing the lovers, is taken up by the huge fruits and the husk-like forms. There is a still clearer distinction between them: on the left spherical structures,

20

in the centre two bursting open, and on the right vertical forms. Some look like many-coloured stones and yet like living growth, others have a glassy appearance (which evoked frequent references to the alchemists' retorts). Erotic initiation may have begun within their walls. Towards the left the symbiosis of vegetable and animal, half immersed in water, becomes more and more insistent. Finally, in front of the barrier of hedge, a flock of enormous birds enter from the left with fixed and penetrating gaze, leaving no impression on the blurred countenances of the naked bathers. The second zone is positively overrun with martial figures. There are several to a group, most of them mounted; they are always distinct from each other and often produce a massed effect. They follow a circular course, but instead of passing through many varied scenes they revolve closely round the central pool where the women are bathing. It is less a rite full of ceremonial gestures than a chase, a roundabout, a carrousel. The madness increases. At last in the third zone it is caught and held in the most bizarre of monuments. In the water floats a spherical construction of definitely technical appearance but for the translucent posts and half-moons set up on it like masts. The four others are rock edifices, part tomb, part tower, part root, as much built as spontaneously arisen. They are not so much lofty towers as a riot of interfused stone, glass, plants and cavities. Attempts at their designation have been made by recourse to astrology or alchemical theory. They are undoubtedly buildings. However much they may seem a natural excrescence or may seem attributable to sexual symbolism, they are in fact determined by those principles of cavity and mortise construction which, apart from their use in painting, were not to attract the technologists and inventors until centuries later.

The hollow globe, observed and exploited as a definite feature (but not an accepted architectural principle until modern times) appears in the picture of Hell on the right-hand panel as an erect figure. From beneath a mill wheel a melancholy countenance peers round its shapeless body at us; the body itself, half shattered egg, half rotten tree, has legs of hollow bark shod with a pair of boats. This shrivelled growth now embodies the quintessence of insecurity – life that has been lost. Bent, oblique, slanting forms lie strewn around. It all began in the world above, with a 'return of the elements to their savage state' (Fraenger), and now a mass of humanity surges along, ingenious in their inventions, hectic in their onslaughts, but few succeed even in reaching the dead tree in this world of emptiness. Those who do actually reach land fall a prey to the torturing musical instruments, or fall amongst an anxious company of dicers. Now all delights are bitter-sweet. Last traces of true delight still linger in those innumerable masochistic, expectant glances which haunt this panel. Neither joy nor torment have an end in such a scene of anguish. The nude figures here are different from the slender, gliding, blissful beings in the enclosed world of plants. Even if they feel desire they remain passive, moving anxiously and timidly towards the scene of their actions, or rather their sufferings.

How shall we define this enormous, perennially captivating picture? Perhaps nothing but a supreme delight in invention has impelled these embodiments of voluptuous tenderness, of horror, exhaustion and extinction. Whether or not they were at the same time programme pictures of a 'Freethinking' sect is an open question. They are at all events – down to the smallest gesture – more astonishing than if they had been mere transcriptions of the rule of life of any such association. Bosch's penetration is surely to be ranked higher than the vitalism of these fraternities, however consecrated. His pictorial sense is greater because instead of turning aside with an air of moral superiority he actually includes in his view of the world not only the loss and distortion of sense but sheer nonsense. One should therefore not look in these pictures for either unity or consistent sense. For it is chance itself that is incorporated into Bosch's symbolism. All things, however fortuitous, are important. Everything which might make sense is simultaneously displayed in crisis and at a moment of decline. It would be unreasonable to expect complete unity and clarity either of composition or of symbolism. The element of chance persists.

Occasionally, however, Bosch probed more deeply into evil than it may seem from this account. This is shown by the torturing, dart-throwing monsters in the fragment of the *Last Judgement* (Plate 68); they have communicated to those risen from the dead such a vision of terror as is usually evoked only by the Judgement itself, as in Michelangelo's *Last Judgement* in the Sistine Chapel. Those visited with annihilation are incomparable figures of naked terror and headlong flight. And they are painted with such certainty of touch on an almost black background that here too a landscape of broad fields can be sensed beyond. Similarly, when looking at the Calendars the eye feels impelled to follow the receding landscape until its outlines are barely distinguishable. These armed, insect-like monsters now merely embody the springs of the action itself; they are hardly symbols, still less spectres. Stylistically the forms belong to the later period; never until the *Garden of Earthly Delights* had they acquired such relief and plasticity.

22

It must be stated at this point that the menacing hybrid creatures are increasingly absent from the later works. They lurk deep down in the blank faces of some of the half-length paintings; for instance the circular picture *The Crowning with Thorns* in the Prado (Plate 70) which shows Christ in the clutches of a boorish soldiery, his pale face looking out at us. The colours almost anticipate Quentin Massys, but they are less luminous, for despite their brilliance they yet retain that dense firm opacity of colour which early characterized Bosch. The Ghent picture of the unruly sea of heads surrounding Christ carrying the Cross, and Saint Veronica (Plates 71–72), is different. Here the dark background is impenetrable and the bright tones of the faces are completely marred by malevolence.

The other way in which the disquieting, suspect, threatening element which had appeared in countless guises disappears from the later works, is by merging into the landscape, as in the *Adoration of the Magi* in the Prado (Plates 74–77). Here, as often with Bosch we can detect in the crumbling house the 'antiquarian' influence of the Master of Flémalle in Dijon. The landscape is silent. The few figures peering oddly from inside the house belong to the Kings' retinue. There are no mechanisms of torture anywhere, except that in the distant landscape we notice surprise attacks and menacing cavalry, or we see on the horizon buildings whose pagoda-like form seems too foreign to bode any good. Has every suspicious feature taken cover in the objects themselves?

It is possible. Bosch forgot nothing. Temptation, the ultimate, fundamental, all-embracing theme of his pictures, reappears in his last works. Formerly the taut figures of Saint Anthony and Saint Jerome held the scale between good and evil. Yet these penitents were at the same time dragged and pulled about, as if benumbed by the fury of the surrounding torments, or as if dead from enduring the blows that rain down on all sides, surrounding and bewildering these tempted saints. Because of this Bosch's paintings never displayed the powers of evil as a mere undisciplined rabble, for the penitent saints provided an unfailing criterion whereby to judge them. That is why any comparison with surrealism is only superficial; behind all the horrifying contrasts, all the clashing incongruities which are intrinsic to surrealism there was always for Bosch the figure who endured them all – and indeed in a manner that seems foreign to the modern mind. Thus temptation recurs in two of his last surviving pictures, but it is hardly instigated by devils. One is the *Prodigal Son* (Plates 78–79), in fact a grisaille with a dull background and dim light. He can hardly be called a son now, for he has gone quite grey.

23

Because of his hunted look, because of various indications at the inn he looks at over his shoulder, and because of the bird-cries along his way, scholars have assumed he is about to return to his father's house. But it is also possible that he has undergone this temptation differently, and that it has taken him all his life to perceive clearly what he has left behind. He has ceased his wanderings but the remoteness of the foreign land prevents his return there. Anyone looking closely at these fine-drawn, lean, careworn features will recognize in them all Bosch's victims of temptation – he is the wanderer, the outcast, condemned to live only in the future. The other picture is the *Temptation of Saint Anthony* in the Prado (Plate 80).

From an easy bird's-eye view we look down on the slender tree-trunks of a lightly wooded valley that consists of almost diagonally arranged surfaces and consistently slanting lines. The Church, the hollow tree and finally the Saint himself all seem to crouch into a ball. And here once more are these mechanism of furious onslaught. But they are so lost, so scattered, so lacking in the atmosphere of menace that usually attends them, that they achieve nothing. And the contemplative saint possesses strength, however much his calm attention is riveted by a horrid apparition peering up from the turbid, lack-lustre stream. Reality itself, despite Bosch's constant sacrifice of phantoms to it, has now itself become sinister.

How did Bosch emerge from this cramped, hostile world of oppressive, rebellious objects? Quite early, as has been seen, his forms seemed smoothly insubstantial, clear of colour. Soon they appeared masked and disguised. But this was only a fragile shell which finally burst open, to reveal his other world within the many-curved hollow interiors. And finally, his landscapes were as clear as a desert. The resulting expanse was less ominous but quite empty so that yet again it looked dangerous. Was the whole of the earth's surface only a thin crust? The paler colours have indeed dispersed much that was repellent. But the old secure Christian themes have also disappeared. Life without fear might now begin, but it can do so only with the legacy of fear which remains imprinted on the soul, a constant companion, as with the later meditative Saint Anthony who has reached the end of his days and awaits death with almost stony indifference.

The really confusing feature of Bosch's painting is that despite all its wealth of realism it strives, almost from the beginning, to express the immaterial. This unusual statement will be understood if one considers how weak, fragile, insubstantial all his figures appear, however true to

24

life they may be. How often is his material world invaded by spirits! But what is his attitude to his own period? He is bound by no new rule, whether classical or scurrilous in the Antwerp manner. It is clear (as in the late *Adoration of the Magi*) that his aim is to express the elemental. But what is the elemental?

In the little raised figures standing out in relief on the metal vessels, in the embroidered pictures on the Kings' robes, he pursues the original shape of the formless yet constructive, but it has crossed the dividing line, it is stamped out of the material itself. Can one tell whether the toads under the vessel resting on the ground are the product of art or nature? Nowadays we should prefer to do quite the contrary and call such things artificial. But soon the time will come when natural discoveries will themselves be called 'artificial'; every rare stone that was mined was displayed to advantage by the jeweller's art, as 'dress rings'. Are they not in fact foreshadowed by the countless stone towers Bosch invented?

What is this product of Bosch's dissatisfaction with everything traditional, crystallized so early, so unswerving in its aim? Why was the ruin of the world through the Fall of Man no longer enough for him? How could he show the *crise de conscience* in the wider field of which he was aware? Not merely through *Ecce homo*, the strange gathering in Cana, Saint Anthony, the hermits, the Prodigal Son, but instead by a sustaining of extremes, a straining after contradictions. That was another matter. The transition into the time he foresaw was difficult for him (hence the considerable archaicism). Do not his pictures reveal, or at least presage, the horror of a 'second nature' (in the sense of technical mastery) and show it growing intimately fused with an active, often painfully aggressive hostile nature (in the sense of life force)?

He distrusted the period in which he grew up. That is why he owed so little to the prevailing ideal, either the eclectic Italian Renaissance or the complex, mysterious Renaissance of the North which produced an unfailing succession of consoling works in Altdorfer, Burgkmair or his own compatriots. Bosch however found his consolation in meditation alone. The idea of this meditation was his conviction, pictorially expressed, that nature's plenitude and excess must point to an inescapable end in the distant future. Bosch painted the early morning of a day which is now drawing to a close. We too can sense that an object, long valid, loses its objectivity and that one approach to the natural sciences can be replaced by another less material one. Morning and evening are as similar as mirror images. But then as today the uncanny mystery they conceal is not only comparable but identical.

25

PLATES

The Seven Deadly Sins and the Four Last Things. Painted Table Top. Madrid, Prado

2. (a) *Death of the Sinner*. (b) *Hell*. Details from Plate 1

3. (a) *The Last Judgement*. (b) *Paradise*. Details from Plate 1

4. (a) *Covetousness; Envy.* (b) *Anger; Pride.* Details from Plate 1

5. *Lust*. Detail from Plate 1

6. (a) *Sloth*. (b) *Gluttony*. Details from Plate 1

7. The Cure of Folly. Madrid, Prado

9. *The Conjurer.* Saint-Germain-en-Laye, Musée municipal

10. *The Adoration of the Magi*. Philadelphia, John G. Johnson Collection

11. Detail from the *Adoration of the Magi* (Plate 10)

12. *The Marriage at Cana*. Rotterdam, Museum Boymans

13. *The Crucifixion*. Brussels, Musées Royaux

14. *Ecce homo*. Frankfurt, Staedel Institute of Art

15. Detail from *Ecce homo* (Plate 14)

16. *The Carrying of the Cross*. Escorial

17. *The Carrying of the Cross*. Vienna, Kunsthistorisches Museum

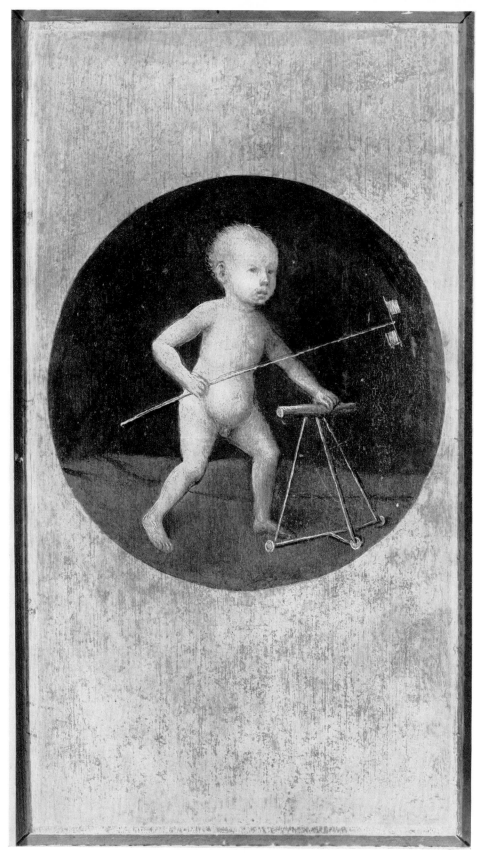

18. *Allegory of Ignorance*. Reverse of Plate 17

). *The Hawker*. Outside of the *Haywain* (Plate 21). Madrid, Prado

20. *Garden of Eden and Hell*. Wings of the *Haywain* (Plate 21)

21. *The Haywain*. Centre panel of the triptych. Madrid, Prado

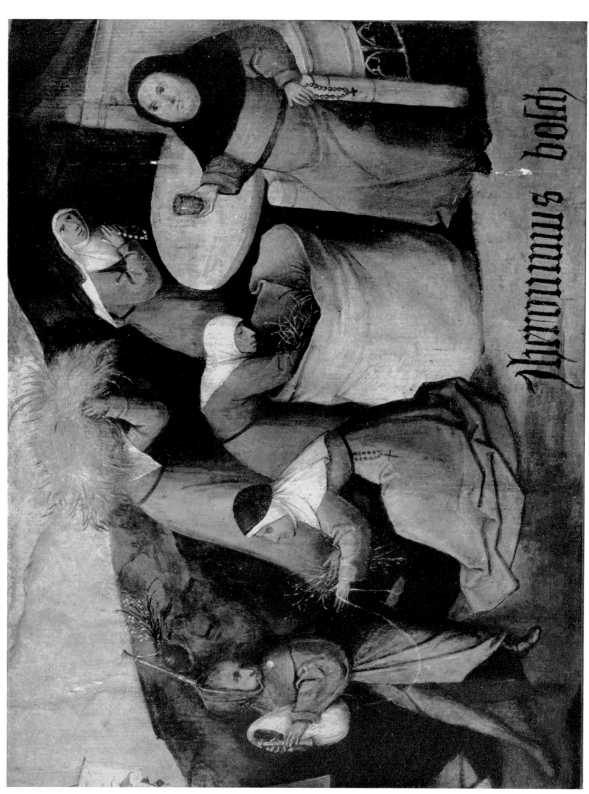

22. Detail from the *Haywain* (Plate 21)

23. Detail from the *Haywain* (Plate 21)

24. Detail from the *Haywain* (Plate 21)

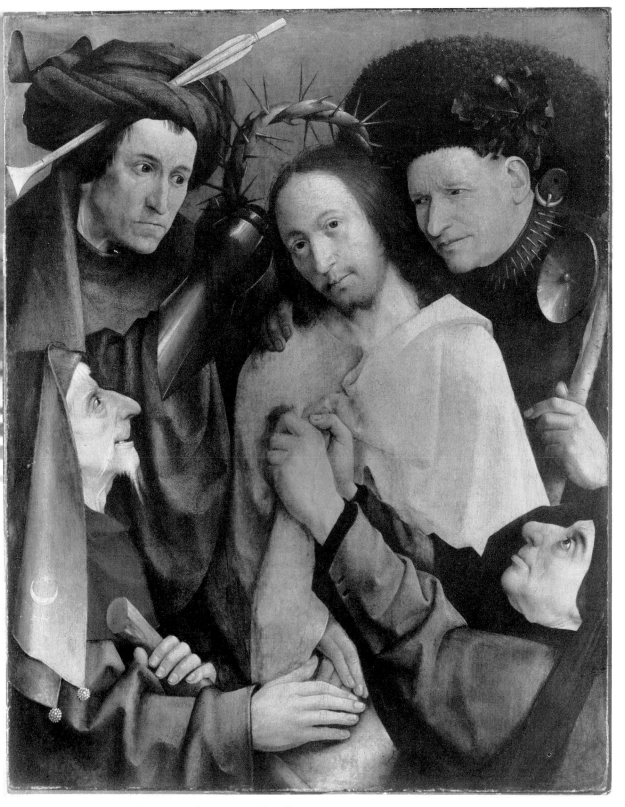

25. *The Crowning with Thorns*. London, National Gallery

26. *Death and the Miser*. Washington, National Gallery of Art, Samuel H. Kress Collection

27. *The Ship of Fools*. Paris, Louvre

28. *Ecce homo*. Philadelphia, John G. Johnson Collection

9. *The Crucifixion of Saint Julia.* On the wings: *The Temptation of Saint Anthony.* Venice, Ducal Palace

30. (a) *The Haunted House.* (b) *The Ploughman and the Devil.* Grisailles.
From the reverse of the *Flood* (Plate 32–a)

31. (a) *The Tribulations of the Soul*. (b) *The Return of the Soul to God*. Grisailles.
From the reverse of the *Flood* (Plate 32–b)

32. *Before and After the Flood*. Grisailles. Rotterdam, Museum Boymans

33. (a) *The Betrayal of Christ.* (b) *The Carrying of the Cross.* Grisailles. Outside of the
  Temptation of Saint Anthony (Plate 41)

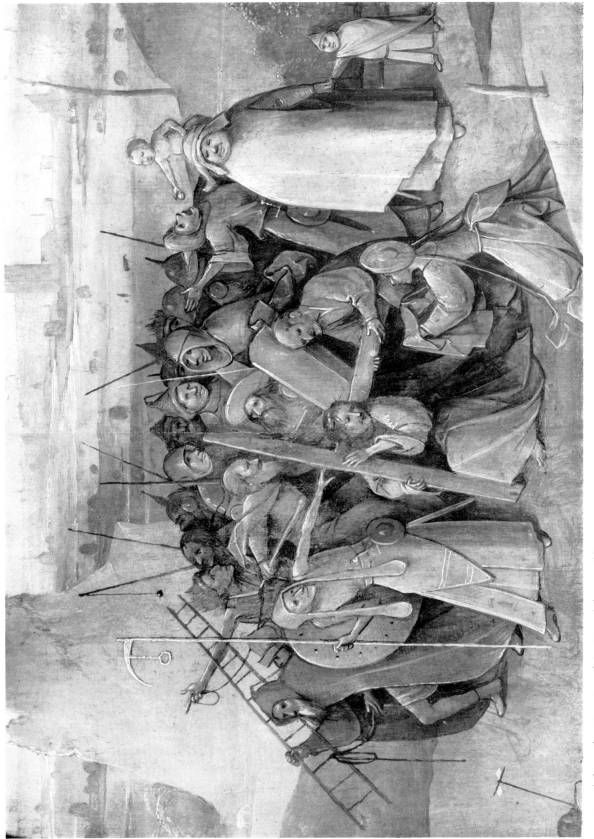

35. Detail from the *Carrying of the Cross* (Plate 33–b)

36. *Two Scenes from the Life of Saint Anthony*. Wings of the *Temptation of Saint Anthony* (Plate 41)

37. Detail from the left wing of the *Temptation of Saint Anthony* (Plate 36–a)

39. Detail from the left wing of the *Temptation of Saint Anthony* (Plate 36–a)

40. Detail from the right wing of the *Temptation of Saint Anthony* (Plate 36–b)

41. *The Temptation of Saint Anthony.* Centre panel of the triptych. Lisbon, Museum of Fine Arts

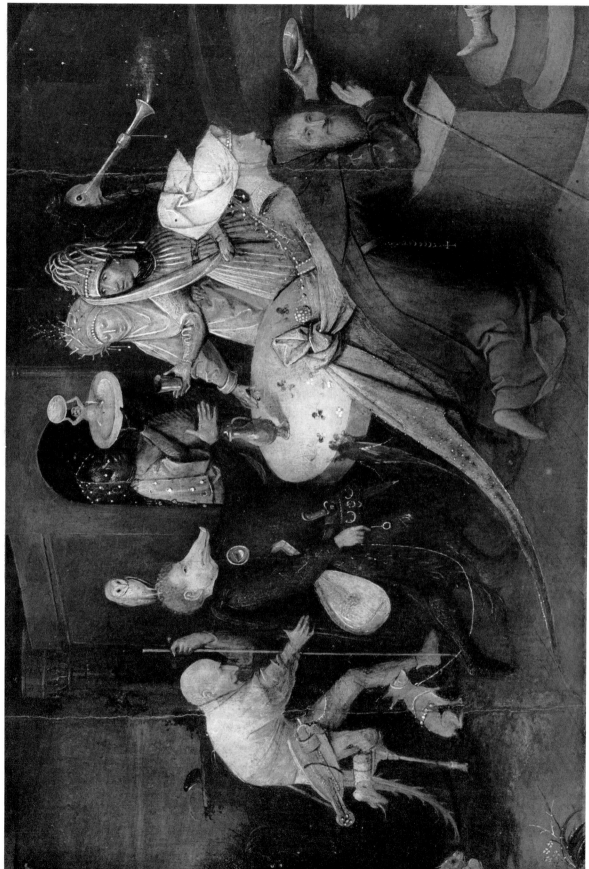

42. Detail from the *Temptation of Saint Anthony* (Plate 41)

43. Detail from the *Temptation of Saint Anthony* (Plate 41)

44. Detail from the *Temptation of Saint Anthony* (Plate 41)

45. Detail from the *Temptation of Saint Anthony* (Plate 41)

46. (a) *The Fall of the Damned.* (b) *Hell.* Venice, Ducal Palace

47. (a) *The Ascent to the Empyrean*. (b) *Paradise*. Venice, Ducal Palace

48. *The Garden of Eden and Hell*. Wings of the *Last Judgement* (Plate 49)

49. *The Last Judgement*. Vienna, Academy of Fine Arts

50. *Altarpiece of the Hermits* (Saints Jerome, Anthony, Giles). Venice, Ducal Palace

51. *Saint Jerome Penitent*. Ghent, Musée des Beaux-Arts

52. *The Passion of Christ*. Grisaille. Reverse of Plate 53

53. *Saint John on Patmos*. Berlin, Museum.

54 Detail from the *Passion of Christ* (Plate 52)

55. Detail from *Saint John on Patmos* (Plate 53)

56. *Saint Christopher*. Rotterdam, Museum Boymans

57. *Saint John the Baptist in the Wilderness*. Madrid, Musco Lazaro Galdiano

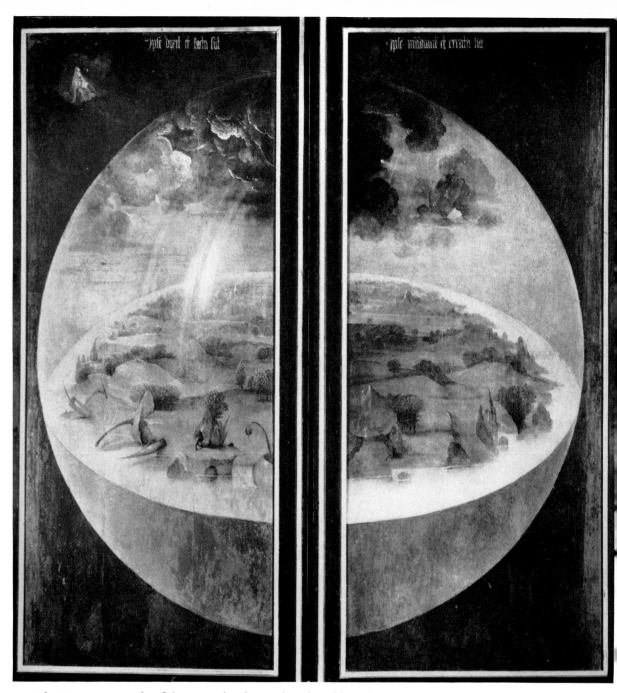

58. *The Creation*. Outside of the triptych *The Garden of Earthly Delights* (Plate 62)

59. (a) *The Garden of Eden.* (b) *Hell.* Wings of the triptych *The Garden of Earthly Delights* (Plate 62)

60. Detail from the *Garden of Eden* (Plate 59–a)

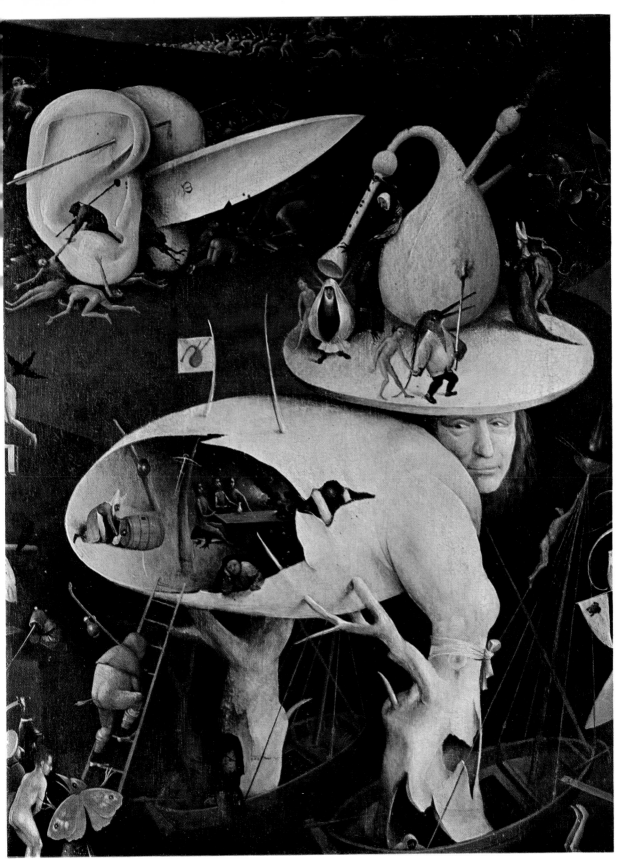

61. Detail from *Hell* (Plate 59–b)

62. *The Garden of Earthly Delights.* Centre panel of the triptych. Madrid, Prado

63. Detail from the *Garden of Earthly Delights* (Plate 62)

64. Detail from the Garden of Earthly Delights (Plate 63)

65. Detail from the *Garden of Earthly Delights* (Plate 62)

67. Detail from the *Garden of Earthly Delights* (Plate 62)

68. *The Last Judgement. Fragment. Munich, Alte Pinakothek*

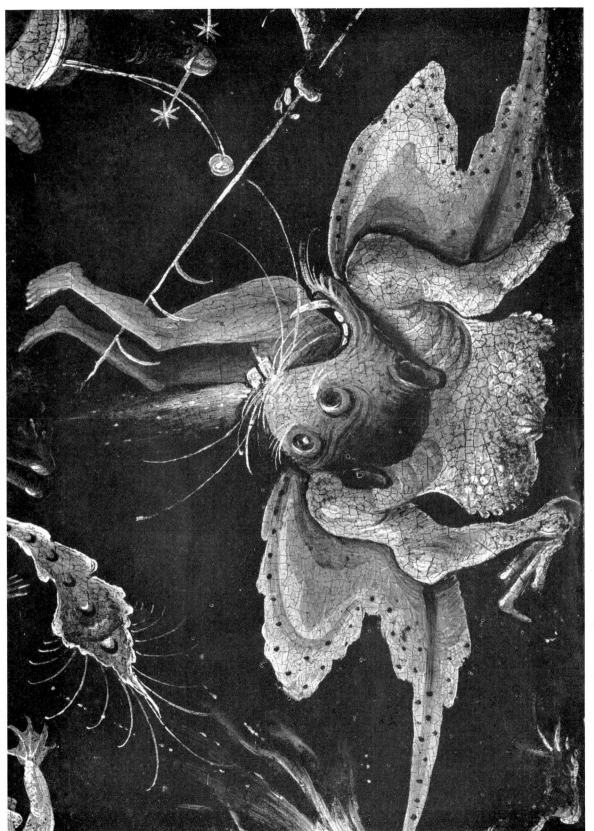

69. Detail from the *Last Judgement* (Plate 68)

70. *The Crowning with Thorns.* Madrid, Prado

71. *The Carrying of the Cross*. Ghent, Musée des Beaux-Arts

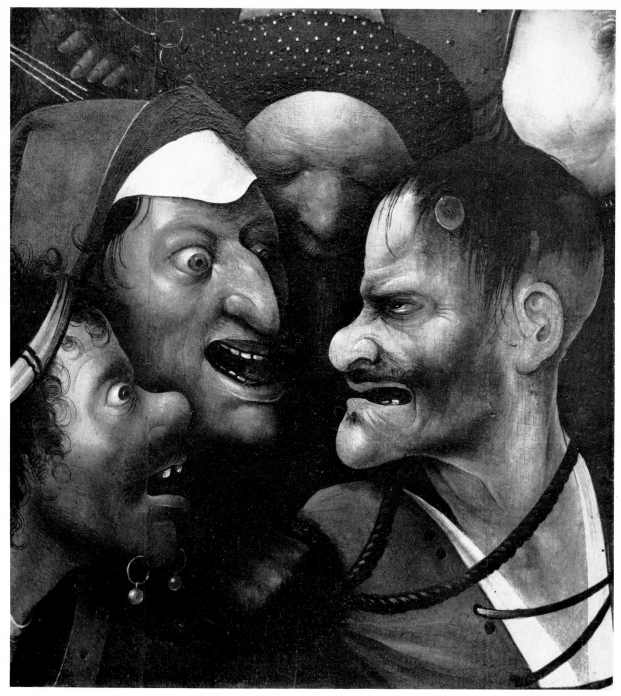

72. *Mocking Mob*. Detail from the *Carrying of the Cross* (Plate 71)

73. *Saint Veronica*. Detail from the *Carrying of the Cross* (Plate 71)

74. *The Adoration of the Magi*. Triptych. Madrid, Prado

75. Detail from the *Adoration of the Magi* (Plate 74)

76. Detail from the *Adoration of the Magi* (Plate 74)

77. *The Mass of Saint Gregory*. Grisaille. Outside of the *Adoration of the Magi* (Plate 74). Madrid, Prado

78. *The Prodigal Son*. Rotterdam, Museum Boymans

79. Detail from the *Prodigal Son* (Plate 78)

80. *The Temptation of Saint Anthony*. Madrid, Prado

NOTES ON THE PLATES

LITERATURE QUOTED IN ABBREVIATED FORM

Max J. Friedländer, *Geertgen und Bosch* (*Die altniederländische Malerei* vol. V). Supplement vol. XIV, Leiden 1937.

Charles de Tolnay, *Hieronymus Bosch*. Basel 1937.

Wilhelm Frænger, *Das Tausendjährige Reich*. Coburg 1947.

Ludwig von Baldass, *Hieronymus Bosch*. Vienna 1943.

Wilhelm Frænger, *Die Hochzeit zu Kana*. Berlin 1950.

Wilhelm Frænger, *Der Tisch der Weisheit, bisher "Die sieben Todsünden" genannt*. Stuttgart 1951.

C. A. Wertheim Aymés, *Hieronymus Bosch, eine Einführung in seine geheime Symbolik*. Amsterdam 1957.

Jacques Combe, *Hieronymus Bosch*. Paris 1946.

NOTES ON THE PLATES

All pictures are painted in oil on wood.

Plates 1–6

THE SEVEN DEADLY SINS AND THE FOUR LAST THINGS

Madrid, Prado. $47\frac{1}{4} \times 59$ in.

In the North, and particularly for Bosch, the circular arrangement known as the tondo held a totally different significance from the one it possessed in Italy. There its purpose was to present a collection of varying scenes, but for Bosch it is a kind of topography, not a guide to the cosmos but an aid in the differentiation and arrangement of moral dicta. The picture, a table top, affects actively and in a variety of ways the people seated round and looking at it; it is not just 'in a frame' (see Tolnay, pp. 17 ff.). The inscriptions on the painting are taken from the Book of Deuteronomy.

2a. *Death of the Sinner.*

2b. *Hell.* Here for the first time Bosch portrays monsters which are not derived from demonic human types but tend towards the quite unfamiliar and indeed mechanical scene of horror. (See Combe, p. 8.)

3a. *The Last Judgement.*

3b. *Paradise.*

4a. *Covetousness; Envy.*

4b. *Anger; Pride.*

5. *Lust.* Baldass' remark about the continuing influence of the 'courtly tone of the Burgundian group of about 1420' should be extended to *Anger* and might also cover the miniatures of the historical codices of Burgundy and indeed of France as a whole.

6a. *Sloth.* The form of this painting may be derived from the pictures of scholars and contemplatives which go back as far as the fourteenth century. But it shows more clearly than the other representations of deadly sins how externally this didactic pictorial fantasy is understood today. For sloth has certainly no connection with mere idleness. *Accidia*, or to give it the purer Latin form, *acedia*, which is nearer to the Greek root,

is a kind of desolate stagnation which often besets precisely those with a religious vocation. To transpose this from the religious to the everyday level, one could hazard this definition: sloth is a disinclination for action which insinuates itself into the greatest and most energetic activity. It is an indolence of the emotions which cannot be explained by mere inactivity. Alone among the critics of Bosch, Combe shows (p. 8) that he appreciates the background of this sin and understands, at least partially, the mordant, inflexible undertone of Bosch's mode of presentation (see Josef Pieper, *Über die Hoffnung*, 3rd edition, Leipzig, 1940, pp. 55–63. Also Walter Benjamin, *Ursprung des Deutschen Trauerspiels*, Berlin 1928, pp. 134 ff., concerning the after-effects of such medieval classification of sins).

6b. *Gluttony.*

Plates 7–8

THE CURE FOR FOLLY

Madrid, Prado. $18\frac{7}{8} \times 13\frac{3}{4}$ in.

Despite many unskilful details this picture already presupposes the picture of the *Deadly Sins*, because of the compositional link between figure and landscape. Proof of this statement must await another occasion. But mention must be made here and now of Tolnay's extraordinary opinion (p. 59, note 26) that this discrepancy renders probable the collaboration of Bosch the Elder. Where? The figures are typical of the younger Bosch, and the landscape is 'progressive'.

Plate 9

THE CONJURER

Saint-Germain-en-Laye, Museum. $20\frac{7}{8} \times 25\frac{5}{8}$ in.

The very people who doubt the authenticity of this picture and call it a copy (however good) have expressed insufficiently founded opinions.

(See Tolnay, p. 18.) However, M. J. Friedländer (vol. V, p. 103) thinks that the significance of this picture goes beyond 'its interpretation as a genre picture ridiculing human stupidity'. In our view it is the vital urgency of the figure painting which differentiates this picture from any notorious copies. Friedländer also tends to regard it as an original. But in his index (p. 152) he says: 'perhaps only an old copy'. Combe expresses no doubts about this picture.

Plates 10–11

THE ADORATION OF THE MAGI

Philadelphia Museum, John G. Johnson Collection.   30½×22 in.

A strangely conventional work but at the same time ecstatic of gesture. Despite constant discussion of this work it still betrays, above all, a similarity with the figures of the Master of the Virgo inter virgines. Combe (p. 80) acutely observes that the picture belongs to the same stage of development as *The Cure of Folly*. (See also Baldass, p. 247.)

Plate 12

THE MARRIAGE AT CANA

Rotterdam, Museum Boymans.   36⅝×28¼ in.

Despite Baldass' penetrating analysis of this picture, it is both indispensable and illuminating to consider Wilhelm Fraenger's observations in *Die Hochzeit zu Kana, ein Dokument semitischer Gnosis bei Hieronymus Bosch*, Berlin 1950 (even though he digresses occasionally). A notable stylistic feature is the principle governing its arrangement, which is nevertheless linked with unrest. It seems to me the earliest approach to the massed mob scene which is so significant in the Frankfurt *Ecce Homo*. But here are two conflicting tendencies, as is shown in the style of painting, alternately inspired or pedestrian.

The picture is in a rather bad state of preservation.

Plate 13

THE CRUCIFIXION

Brussels, Musées Royaux.   29×24⅛ in.

Here too the somewhat inhibited gestures have a flat, archaic, almost disguised quality. But for the first time the landscape claims the attention in quite a different way, with its unusual, dreamlike buildings and at times the sharp outlines of shrivelled vegetation. (See Combe, p. 81.)

Plates 14–15

ECCE HOMO

Frankfurt, Staedel Institute of Art.   29½×24 in.

This picture displays the spiritualization of the material world which is so constant a feature of Bosch's later work. It persists throughout Bosch's development, increasing still further the painter's invention. Tolnay says (p. 16): 'The figures, deprived of their plasticity and weight, assume an unreal air which is the more disturbing in that their tightly packed mass seems to burst out of the frame and become a vision of the whole of humanity.'

Plate 16

THE CARRYING OF THE CROSS

Escorial.   59×37 in.

In contrast to most of Bosch's early or later canvases, traversed by such cavalcades of figures, this picture is characterized by its smooth, undulating relief, mainly because of the folds in the draperies. This is, however, a larger, more monumental treatment of surface areas than usual which is reminiscent of Schongauer, whose influence is elsewhere perceived only in details.

Plates 17–18

THE CARRYING OF THE CROSS

Vienna, Kunsthistorisches Museum. 22½×12⅝ in.

See Baldass (pp. 45–46 and especially p. 61) for this treatment in two overlapping bands and for the archaic origins of this arrangement. The still considerable smooth mobility of all the faces seems to me to make impossible Tolnay's dating of this picture after the *Haywain*. But see Combe p. 19 for the temporal proximity of both pictures.

18. *Allegory of Ignorance*. Reverse of plate 17. Because the front of this picture shows the fateful end of Christ's life, there is scant sense in seeing in this lad an earlier stage of that same life, or comfortably adopting professional jargon and talking of 'the Christ Child at play'. The death of

the two condemned criminals in the picture, rare in scenes other than the Passion, is to be taken as entirely profane. The significance of the child, too, is profane: the allegory of ignorance. And the conspicuous clarity of the instruments indicates allegory.

Plates 19–24
TRIPTYCH: THE HAYWAIN

Madrid, Prado.

Central Panel: 53⅛×39⅜ in. Each wing: 53⅛× 17¾ in.

19. *The Hawker* (Outside of the Haywain). It will be difficult to find the fitting designation for this man who is usually called 'tramp' or 'vagrant'. But once again, why this tendency to 'explain' in terms of a genre? The man's peculiarly gliding bent-kneed gait has a strange ceremonial quality. Moreover it recurs so often in Bosch's pictures like a rite – in *Saint Christopher* (56) and also in *The Prodigal Son* (78). And it is well known that the thought content of Bosch's pictures owes much to writings on moral theology. This seems to me the visible manifestation of the traditional figure of the *homo viator*. This 'journey undertaken' is the journey through sin; and the many varieties of such journeys form Bosch's constant theme. *The Haywain* is more explicit about this than any other picture. And Saint Augustine, who called human birth the beginning of death, was one of the favourite sources of Bosch's contemporaries. Thus here the *homo viator* progresses against a backcloth of painful, or at least thoroughly disturbed existence. The turbulent or dangerous scenes and the débris which life has scattered over the landscape, are not a vague record but the very attributes of such a pilgrim as this.

20. *Garden of Eden and Hell*. We ought perhaps to spend far less trouble (usually fruitless) on comparing the various punishments for sin in the wing of *Hell* with the older representation of Hell in the *Deadly Sins* and on endeavouring more or less to identify them. Such zeal seems to me useless in comparison with the awareness of motifs which have not occurred hitherto and are so very terrifying for precisely the reason that they are incomparable. One may perhaps cite, as an example, the naked man in the procession of evil, who is addressed unexpectedly by a stag with human hind legs but his own forelegs – a 'diversion' which only doubles the misery. And then, just beside him, the cloaked man rattling along with a gigantic bridle bit seems almost in pain and stamps sullenly on. One should not aim at describing features as fully as possible, but at noting what their first appearance reveals about Bosch's inner development. The stage is now reached at which perdition for him is not represented by the sight of human wickedness. Rather do the tormentors inflict torture and undergo suffering simultaneously, and the victims combine anxiety and peace of mind. This will later become his private symbolism.

21. Centre panel: *The Haywain*. It is fascinating to notice that here the colour of fertility, of ripeness, of bread, which is also the colour of the desert, is accorded the central place, circumscribed and almost 'encroached on' – the same colour which in his later works becomes the basis and extent of the tranquillity portrayed.

Plate 25
THE CROWNING WITH THORNS

London, National Gallery. 29×23¼ in.

Here again the same curious broad surface areas prevail, together with the soft reliefs (as in the *Carrying of the Cross* in the Escorial) which could point to an early or late period. (See Combe, pp. 44 and 94.)

Plate 26
DEATH AND THE MISER

Washington, National Gallery of Art, Samuel H. Kress Collection. 36⅝×12¼ in.

Cracks and trapdoors are the basic forms in the perspective of this picture. In the foreground lies a confusion of scattered objects, and then begins this tendency common to the North Netherlands school (not only in one wing of the *Haywain*) to open holes down to the 'lower regions'. (See Combe, p. 20.)

Plate 27
THE SHIP OF FOOLS

Paris, Louvre. 22×12⅝ in.

Despite Combe's contribution to the correct interpretation of this picture (pp. 21–22) by his citing of various motifs from Sebastian Brant's 'Ship of Fools' the decisive contribution comes from Tolnay (p. 27) who mentions those lines of verse by Brant which almost describe this picture: how often we wander in quest of harbour and shore, never finding a quayside where we may land, so that our vain drifting hardly has an end.

Plate 28
ECCE HOMO
Philadelphia, John G. Johnson Collection.
$20\frac{1}{2} \times 21\frac{1}{4}$ in.

The unusual style of painting in this picture requires particular reflection before assigning it a date, which has been done most successfully by Combe (pp. 24, 85). But the most fitting description is Tolnay's (p. 21).

Plate 29
TRIPTYCH: THE CRUCIFIXION OF SAINT JULIA
Venice, Ducal Palace.
Centre Panel: $41 \times 24\frac{3}{4}$ in. Each Wing: 41×11 in.

In this picture, more than any other of Bosch's later works, the flowing movement and interlocking of the figures is significant. It is no longer the hard mob grouping of the earlier pictures and is not yet the many-coloured suppleness of the works following the Lisbon Triptych. This is why I should like to differ from Combe (p. 90) and place the work before the Lisbon *Saint Anthony*. The rich colours are both soft and vivid and seem to me to parallel those of the splendid Crucifixion Triptych by the Master of the Virgo inter Virgines (Barnard Castle), despite the difference arising from the fact that the figures on the Saint Julia altarpiece are three times smaller. A second cardinal point is that these strongly individual colours contain the picture's closely concealed exoticism. For example, the pagoda tower with a conical roof shown from above on the right wing, and the 'Chinese' to the right of the centre panel, himself a pagoda, built with meticulous smoothness, around his body a frieze showing fighting dragons. This triptych has suffered from fire and is in a very bad state of preservation.

Plates 30–32
BEFORE AND AFTER THE FLOOD
Rotterdam, Museum Boymans.
Left Wing: $27\frac{7}{8} \times 14\frac{1}{8}$ in. Right Wing: $27\frac{7}{8} \times 15$ in.

30. Reverse of the Left Wing. (a) *Haunted House*. (b) *The Ploughman and the Devil*. All necessary commentary on this and the following side of the picture may be found in Fraenger's *Hochzeit*, pp. 11–19, 99–107.
31. Reverse of the Right Wing. (a) *The Tribulations of the Soul*. (b) *The Return of the Soul to God*.
32. Left Wing: *The Descendants of the Fallen Angels*. Right Wing: *The Ark*.

Plates 33–45
TRIPTYCH: THE TEMPTATION OF SAINT ANTHONY
Lisbon, Museum of Fine Arts.
Centre panel: $51\frac{3}{4} \times 46\frac{7}{8}$ in. Each Wing: $51\frac{3}{4} \times 20\frac{7}{8}$ in.

The sublime colours of this altarpiece with their distinctively ethereal quality which emerges despite all the eloquent urgency of colour and which points in turn to the immateriality or, better, the weakening of all objective solidity in the later works, are best described by Tolnay (p. 28). As regards the interpretation of various secret signs, one should consult Fraenger's rambling if telling remarks scattered at random in *Hochzeit*, pp. 47, 61–65 (with 54), 72, 83, 89 *et seq.*

Plates 46–47
WINGS OF AN ALTARPIECE
Venice, Ducal Palace.
Each Wing: $34 \times 15\frac{1}{2}$ in.

46. (a) *The Fall of the Damned*. (b) *Hell*.
47. (a) *The Ascent to the Empyrean*. (b) *The Garden of Eden*.
These four grisailles are rather badly preserved. In view of the unusual heaven motif, Combe (p. 23) pointed to a mystical source, namely, Ruysbroeck. The nearest comparable painting to the finely brushed, luminous delicacy of form shown by the angels is found in the contemporary works of Geertgen tot Sint Jans (which are small in format).

Plates 48–49

THE LAST JUDGEMENT

Vienna, Academy of Fine Arts.

Centre Panel: $64\frac{1}{8} \times 50\frac{1}{4}$ in. Wings: $65\frac{3}{4} \times 23\frac{5}{8}$ in.

48. *Paradise and Hell*. Wings.

49. Centre Panel. *The Last Judgement*. There has long been considerable disagreement about the attribution of this triptych to Bosch. (See Robert Eigenberger, Descriptive Catalogue of the Gallery of the Academy, Vienna 1927, pp. 50 *et seq*. Also the particularly powerful defence by Max J. Friedländer of the picture's authenticity in *Die Altniederländische Malerei*, vol. V, pp. 99–100.) I should myself prefer to accept Ludwig Goldscheider's opinion. He regards this work (as he has kindly informed me) as partly authentic. The lower part of the centre panel is, he thinks, manifestly by Bosch, but the upper part is hard to judge since it suffered the most by fire (or by the heat of the altar candles). Further, the wings, *Paradise* and *Hell*, are probably by the same assistant who painted the *Last Judgement* in the Cathedral at Tudela (in Spain). In addition to Friedländer, Glück, Hymans and L. Münz declared it authentic – the latter even after the picture was recently cleaned; Baldass was undecided (p. 241), but more recently he has declared them to be authentic (Catalogue of the Vienna Academy, 1957, I, p. 14); Goldscheider sees it as a painting done in the workshop with the collaboration of the master. The outer wings in grisaille (*St. James the Elder as a Pilgrim* and *Saint Bavo*) are (again according to Goldscheider) not by Bosch, perhaps only copies based on drawings by him. Baldass (quoted in the Catalogue of the Vienna Academy, I, 1957, p. 14) now regards these outer wings as by Bosch's own hand. They are most accurately rendered, since they display unusual delicacy for the hand of a copyist. In addition there are several notable stylistic features, for example the bent-kneed gait of the pilgrim James (see plates 19, 56, 78) and on the other wing the curiously piled up group at the right with the woman's head in profile and at the left the flayed and amputated foot on a linen cloth. (Cf. plate 42). See here p. 116; Combe, p. 84; and, in particular, Ludwig Münz, Catalogue of the Vienna Academy, 1957, I, pp. 7–14.

Plate 50

TRIPTYCH:
ALTARPIECE OF THE HERMITS

Venice, Ducal Palace.

Centre Panel: $34 \times 23\frac{5}{8}$ in. Each Wing: $34 \times 11\frac{3}{8}$ in.

Since the ascetic ideal of the high Middle Ages changed in Bosch's day and since a new one can be formed only by renewed experience of this vain world, the resulting asceticism of these friars is almost entirely spiritual. Tolnay (p. 37), basing himself on Saint Jerome, says that the Saint is not praying but is trying to reconcile the contradictory visions which extend further and further the contemplative drama of his life. That is no doubt why the picture is full of signs of experience of the world and its widespread heresies. An idolater, a sun-worshipper, almost hidden away in a retort; a 'secret' known but not respected. Behind it another topples down and falls on what remains of the magnificent tessellated ('heathen') floor. This triptych is in a bad state of preservation.

Plate 51

SAINT JEROME PENITENT

Ghent, Musée des Beaux-Arts. $30\frac{1}{4} \times 23\frac{1}{4}$ in.

On the possible dates of this picture, see Combe, p. 94 (he refuses to place it before the *Garden of Earthly Delights*) and Baldass, p. 244 (before the Lisbon Saint Anthony altarpiece).

Plates 52–55

SAINT JOHN ON PATMOS

Berlin, Museum. $24\frac{1}{2} \times 16\frac{1}{8}$ in.

52. *The Passion of Christ. Grisaille. Reverse of Plate 53*. The circular tondo, the 'eye of God' does not this time contain within the pupil the figure of Christ who interprets the sins exemplified in the iris. Instead wide horizons can be seen in both circles – the inner one contains a rocky island on the top of which a pelican tends its young, and in the circular band of the iris this Passion landscape sinks lower and lower so as to merge into the blurred outlines of rocky ravines

St. James the Elder as a Pilgrim and St. Bavo. Grisailles. Outside of the wings of the
Last Judgement. Vienna, Academy of Fine Arts.

and cave constructions – the Mount of Olives and the Sepulchre.

53. *Saint John on Patmos.* (For description and dating see Combe, pp. 36 and 91.)

Plate 56
SAINT CHRISTOPHER

Rotterdam, Museum Boymans. $44\frac{1}{2} \times 28\frac{1}{8}$ in.

To arrive at some understanding of this highly enigmatic picture one must consult Baldass (pp. 34 *et seq.* and 244) and Fraenger (in *Hochzeit*, pp. 110–114), although the latter, scorning plain description of a picture's 'mood', can only see this one in terms of a genre, but he does place it very high in pictures of sectarian life.

Plate 57
SAINT JOHN THE BAPTIST IN THE WILDERNESS

Madrid, Museo Lázaro Galdiano. $19\frac{1}{8} \times 15\frac{3}{4}$ in.

Tolnay (p. 38) gives an unusual and most revealing description of this picture. He compares the fabulous plant, that symbol of sensual delights, with the rod of Jesse and sees the Saint unconsciously pointing to the lamb, confronted with the choice between the good and the evil path.

Plates 58–67
TRIPTYCH: THE GARDEN OF EARTHLY DELIGHTS

Madrid, Prado. Centre panel, $86\frac{5}{8} \times 76\frac{3}{4}$ in.

58. *The Creation.* Outside of the Triptych. The circular form again, this time not the 'eye of God' but a transparent globe. Thus it is a bird's-eye picture of creation. (See Combe, p. 71, notes 114 and 115.)

Plates 68–69
THE LAST JUDGEMENT

Munich, Alte Pinakothek. Fragment, $23\frac{5}{8} \times 44\frac{7}{8}$ in.

The style of this picture is ecstatic throughout, as incisive as it is delicate. The bird-man's yellow sleeves (top right) can be instanced as 'late' because of the complexity of their brush work, as can the plastic, phosphorescent costumes of the group at the bottom right. In addition, the

assured, impenetrable expressions, whether realistic or grotesque, point clearly to that concentration of form which characterizes Bosch's latest work. Similarly, as Tolnay points out (p. 35), both the great and the humble of this world try to hide their face with the same common gesture of despair.

Plate 70
THE CROWNING WITH THORNS

Madrid, Prado. $65 \times 76\frac{3}{4}$ in.

Despite many basic characteristics of Bosch's style, the colours seem strange – not only because of the pale gold ground. Strong colours are combined with pale ones, and this again is typical of Bosch when painting, as here, a 'memorial' of great models. In doing so, he does not appear eclectic, can never be confused with any earlier period, but is in a profound sense 'archaic'. That is, he quotes and yet conceals the fact.

Plates 71–73
THE CARRYING OF THE CROSS

Ghent, Musée des Beaux-Arts. $29\frac{1}{8} \times 31\frac{7}{8}$ in.

One might at first think that Bosch had in this picture returned to the conception of his earliest works in which all evil lay hidden in the human countenance, and there was no trace of the materialized ghouls of his future life's work. Here again, these demons are not stalking around openly, but are shown as human faces. But even here one remembers for the first time an almost exact contemporary of his, Leonardo da Vinci. Not only did he see and portray similar monsters in human shape; he too, like Bosch, practised the sceptical approach of statement without commentary. They have no doubt much more in common, for example they neither of them press on to a goal, but remain on the outskirts of their theme because it is too presumptuous to hope to reach its centre. In the *Garden of Earthly Delights* Bosch resembles Leonardo in that he invents experimental forms (though of an entirely anti-realistic nature) which strive to master the threatening element (see Fraenger, pp. 37 and 68). Then indeed everything withdraws again until we have the calm of the later *Saint Anthony* (Prado).

Plates 74–77
TRIPTYCH:
THE ADORATION OF THE MAGI

Madrid, Prado.

Centre Panel: $54\frac{3}{8} \times 28\frac{1}{4}$ in. Each Wing: $54\frac{3}{8} \times$ 13 in.

See Combe (pp. 45 ff. and 94 ff.) on this picture seen as an allegory of the Mass. Similarly Tolnay (pp. 43 ff.).

Plates 78–79
THE PRODIGAL SON

Rotterdam, Museum Boymans. Diameter $27\frac{3}{4}$ in.

Tolnay (p. 71, note 149), has no doubt what the subject matter is but he points out (p. 72, note 153) that there is an element of the old basic pattern of 'The Choice of Hercules'. (See also

Fraenger in the Amsterdam periodical *Castrum Peregrini* I, 1951, pp. 27–39; finally in *Hochzeit*, pp. 108–110.)

Plate 80
THE TEMPTATION OF SAINT ANTHONY

Madrid, Prado. $27\frac{1}{2} \times 20\frac{1}{8}$ in.

The immateriality of this 'weightless world' is described by Tolnay (p. 45) who adds an observation on the 'fixity' of this contemplative Saint, supported by a passage from Ruysbroeck. Fraenger, in a monograph on this *Temptation*, goes one step in a completely contrary direction; he claims to see in the mask-like reflection in the stream the actual onslaught of the Tempter which he describes by reference to C. G. Jung, *Archivio di Filosofia* (Enrico Castelli, Padua 1957); in particular pp. 160–163.

INDEX OF PLACES